THE LITTLE BOOK OF
TAKE THAT

THE LITTLE BOOK OF
TAKE THAT

Written by Ian Welch

THE LITTLE BOOK OF
TAKE THAT

This edition first published in the UK in 2007
By Green Umbrella Publishing

© Green Umbrella Publishing 2007

www.greenumbrella.co.uk

Publishers Jules Gammond and Vanessa Gardner

Printed and bound in China

ISBN: 978-1-905828-90-6

Contents

Chapter 1

The Take That Phenomenon

GARY BARLOW, HOWARD DONALD, Jason Orange, Mark Owen and Robbie Williams each possess, in their separate ways, unquestioned talents. When these talents were merged together in 1990 under the banner of Take That, the mixture became explosive. And in the new century, after the echoes of this explosion had all but died away, the first four of these have got back together again to show that the old charge remains.

To scale the heights that Take That did in their first coming is almost unprecedented. However, to leave the stage for ten years and then to return to achieve equivalent success is truly phenomenal, especially when conventional wisdom dictates that boy bands who have acquired a teenage girl audience rarely, if ever, maintain their appeal. Their fans retain a little sentiment, sure, but do they still go on record-buying sprees as they did before? Not as a rule.

Because, it has to be admitted, the singers in the band had set the bar incredibly high for themselves. Selling over 20 million records in the first half of the 1990s was a colossal achievement. Their albums ("Everything Changes", "Nobody Else" and "Greatest Hits") all made it to the Number 1 spot, with the sole exception of their debut "Take That And Party", which went to Number 2. They also had eight chart-topping singles, the first

THE TAKE THAT PHENOMENON

LEFT Take That were originally put together to be the UK's answer to New Kids on the Block

THE TAKE THAT PHENOMENON

RIGHT Robbie's bad ways, were not always the right image for a boy band

four that went straight to the top in succession, a feat not achieved since those heady days of the 1960s when the Beatles were in their pomp.

As for their concert appearances, they had provoked a similar brand of hysteria to Beatlemania. It was during their shows that the couple of years the band spent honing their craft in the hard-to-please discos and gay bars bore fruit. They had learned how to whip up a storm with almost every type of audience, and were able to maintain their professionalism, in the midst of scenes of wild enthusiasm, to thrilling effect.

What was the Take That thrill founded upon? Like most good formulas, it was an essentially simple one. The group was unashamedly based on a desire to entertain. A potent blend of Hi-NRG disco foot-stompers and crowd-pleasing light rockers provided the excitement while the soaring ballads drove arrows straight to the hearts of their following. Every song aimed to stimulate the primary emotions, and the band members became masters at hitting the right spot.

Such success always exerts a price. Strains within the group began to show. Their manager Nigel Martin-Smith had notoriously imposed a regime of almost monastic seclusion upon the young superstars. No girlfriends were allowed, drugs were completely forbidden and some of the highest earners in showbiz were confined to receiving spending money of £150 each week. Admittedly, the group found some of these restrictions easy enough to evade and there were quite a few stories in the press of wild nights which didn't always involve supermodels and Robbie. Nevertheless they were, to a greater or lesser extent, chafing at the bit and it seemed to be getting some of them down.

Robbie Williams was the first to let the pressures affect him badly. His behaviour grew more erratic and his utterances more divisive. A much-publicised binge with the members of Oasis at the Glastonbury Festival in June 1995 proved to be the straw that broke the camel's back. It became a question of whether he'd leave before he was pushed. A press conference on 17 July 1995 announced that he was no longer in the band.

It was the beginning of the end. Although the four remaining members soldiered on as successfully as before, the magic had somehow gone. Although

THE TAKE THAT PHENOMENON

FAR RIGHT Robbie was hitting the self-destruct button with his binge drinking

RIGHT The band shortly after Robbie departed

rumours of an impending split were consistently denied, another press conference on 13 February 1996 confirmed that they were true. Emergency hotlines were set up to deal with the frenzied calls of distraught fans. One more chart-topping single and an album of greatest hits and the group had gone.

The critics predicted great things for all the five original members of the band, but curiously it was only Robbie, who had jumped ship first, who fulfilled these expectations. His solo career has been wondrously successful, a battery of great songs backed by an ever-present willingness to explore and confront his demons make him consistently fascinating to the public. Maybe it was because he was, at least superficially, the one happiest in the spotlight.

By contrast, Gary, the main songwriter, began with two Number 1 solo singles, but gradually withdrew from public gaze, partly due to critical reaction, until it seemed he was content to be a power behind the scenes, concentrating on his writing. Although an enviable record for lesser stars, it was not quite the meteoric ascent people assumed he would make.

THE TAKE THAT PHENOMENON

RIGHT The four
members of Take That
announce their
Ultimate Tour, 2006

ABOVE Take That, The Ultimate Collection – Never Forget, Nov 2005

the group imploded drew to a close, there was talk of a TV documentary to tell the story. Surprisingly, everyone, including Robbie, agreed to take part. Less surprisingly, people agreed that, if there was an audience for a TV show, there might also be a market for another album release.

"The Ultimate Collection – Never Forget" was released in November 2005 to mark the 10 years since the band split up. Not many albums can boast such a roster of Number 1 singles, with the exception of Take That's "Greatest Hits" of which this was a virtual repackaging. "Today I've Found You", an aptly-named newly found track from the archives (earmarked originally as a follow-up to "Back For Good") was the only addition.

Otherwise the hits rolled back the years. "How Deep Is Your Love", "Never Forget", "Back For Good", "Sure", "Love Ain't Here Anymore", "Everything Changes", "Babe", "Relight My Fire", "Pray", "Why Can't I Wake Up With You", "Could It Be Magic", "A Million Love Songs", "I Found Heaven", "It Only Takes A Minute", "Once You've Tasted Love", "Promises", "Do What You Like", and "Love Ain't Here Anymore" (US

Similarly, Mark started with a couple of Top 3 singles, but also faded from public consciousness – until he won *Celebrity Big Brother* in 2002. Jason took up acting for a while but felt unfulfilled and Howard became a DJ with a growing reputation in England and on Continental Europe. And there it seemed the amazing story might end.

But anniversaries are very important in the showbiz world. As a decade since

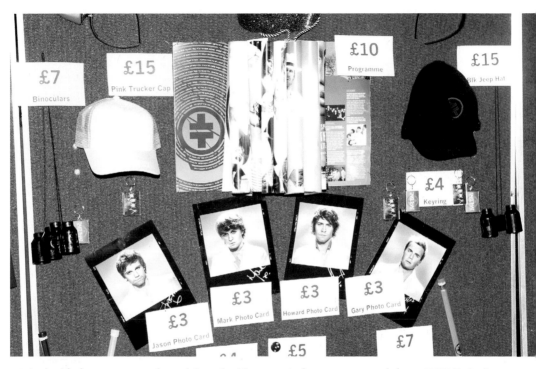

£7
Binoculars

£15
Pink Trucker Cap

£10
Programme

£15
Blk Jeep Hat

£4
Keyring

£3
Jason Photo Card

£3
Mark Photo Card

£3
Howard Photo Card

£3
Gary Photo Card

£5

£7

version) with the new song at the end. It reversed the order of their hits and, one more time, they struck a chord with the record-buying public. The album peaked at Number 2. So far, so good.

Such was the spontaneous outpouring of emotion released by the ending of the 10-year wait that a tour seemed the next logical step. Gary, Howard, Jason and Mark (everyone bar Robbie, in fact) indicated they were all up for it.

The tour was instantly a sell-out and the group had to keep adding date after date to satisfy demand. Nor did they

ABOVE Merchandise from the Ultimate Tour in 2006

THE TAKE THAT PHENOMENON

disappoint their eager audiences. Although everyone involved had inevitably grown up in the intervening years, the response was no less enthusiastic for being more considered. It was (almost) just like the old days – except for the fact that rumours of Robbie joining them on stage remained unfulfilled. Except for the hologram.

However, the acid test was whether they could write a body of new songs that would capture the public imagination. On 9 May 2006, the group signed a deal with Polydor Records. This time around, all the members of the group (and even some outsiders) assisted in the songwriting, taking some of the burden from Gary. There were more rumours that Robbie might return, but no dice.

The first single, "Patience", with Gary on lead vocal, was released at the end of November 2006. It shot to Number 1 and indeed worked its way into the affections of the record-buying public so comprehensively that it was voted the Best British Single of 2006 at the Brit Awards.

So this is where the story stands today. Yet where did it begin?

THE TAKE THAT PHENOMENON

LEFT Back for good!

Chapter 2

Forming the Perfect Boy Band

IN 1990, MANCHESTER WAS AT THE heart of the UK's music scene. Wherever one went, the Manchester sound with its novel mixture of reggae, dance and rock was predominant. Bands such as the Stone Roses, Happy Mondays, Inspiral Carpets and the Charlatans were the names on the lips of music fans. But for one man in the Manchester entertainment industry, it was not enough.

Nigel Martin-Smith had noticed that, although record sales for these bands were reasonable enough, they were not massive. To achieve that level, he reckoned, any group would have to have crossover potential, avoiding the increasingly narrow definitions into

which the music business was falling. In short, for a group to be staggeringly successful, it had to be a pure pop group.

With the appeal of Bros starting to fade, there was only one such group around at that time. New Kids on the Block had been the first boy band import from the USA since the teeny-bop days of the Osmonds and David Cassidy in the early 1970s. They had just had two Number 1 hit singles in the UK with "You Got It (The Right Stuff)" and "Hangin' Tough". A British version was called for, according to Martin-Smith, and, in particular, a Manchester version.

This conclusion happened to chime in with his background. He was a show-biz man. He had cut his teeth in the casting side of the entertainment business, and he set about fulfilling his vision in the way he knew best. He began to cast the parts of the boys in the band.

The first essentials were to have a sensitive singer and an extremely good-looking one. Fortunately he had the pair on his books under the name of the Cutest Rush. The sensitive singer-songwriter was Gary Barlow who had been playing in clubs for several years already. While recording at Manchester's Strawberry Studios, he had met Mark Owen, a former child model and Manchester United triallist, who was working there as a teaboy. The two got on well and formed a duo, singing Gary's songs and a few covers.

Some good movers were also vital to the band's success. Jason Orange and Howard Donald were both dancers who admired each other's styles and had formed the dance duo, Streetbeat. When they approached Martin-Smith, he put them together with Gary and Mark. The nucleus of the band was formed.

But there was one other ingredient crucial to making it all go with a zing – a cheeky chappie, and this time there wasn't one on tap. Advertisements were

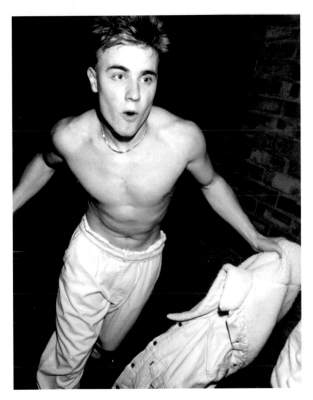

duly placed in the trade magazines. Robbie Williams had been a child actor (whose biggest role had aptly been the Artful Dodger in *Oliver*), and he attended the auditions after his

mother had spotted the advertisement. Everybody immediately knew he was right, and he got the part.

However, beyond casting, there was no actual blueprint for chart domination. There wasn't even a name for a start. Various ideas were put forward, and at one time it even looked as if the group were about to be called Kick It. Fortunately, this was ditched and they settled on Take That, apparently inspired by an article on Madonna, then at the height of her powers and her establishment-baiting fame. What they were all agreed upon was that they wanted to be a pure pop band.

Next they had to address the problem of building up a fan base. Teenage girls (and younger) were an obvious target audience, but the teen magazines proved surprisingly resistant to the group at first. So Martin-Smith had to fall back on known ground and they began to build a reputation in the gay clubs and bars. It certainly helped that they were all natural performers (in Gary's case, with a storehouse of experience) but nevertheless it was a hard training ground.

So, too, were the schools and under-18 clubs where the group sweated to broaden their appeal. However, such hard work eventually began to pay off. The band had been noticed and they were signed to RCA Records in 1991.

Any hopes that the group were about to become an overnight sensation soon stalled. The first single, "Do What You Like", despite (or because of) being famously hyped by a video of the ever-

FORMING THE PERFECT BOY BAND

early 1990s) but a showbiz enthusiast. He had had a clear vision of the group he wanted to see, and cast them superbly, but no real yardsticks by which to develop their potential.

The next single, "Promises", did marginally better, reaching Number 38 in its two-week spell in the charts in November 1991. The third, "Once You've Tasted Love", lasted a week longer, but peaked at Number 47 in February 1992. It was a case of one step forward, one step back. Obviously the group had something but they didn't seem quite able to express it on record – or at least the public had yet to take the bait. It's arguable whether today's harassed music business executives, driven by corporate demands and the instant expectations of reality shows, would have kept faith for so long.

It was the release of the cover version of the old Tavares hit, "It Only Takes A Minute", that unlocked the door. Staying in the charts for eight weeks, it rose as high as Number 7. This was even higher than the original had reached (Top 10 in the US in 1975, Top 50 in the UK in 1986). There was collective joy and relief all round.

The breakthrough was at hand.

willing members of the band rolling around in jelly, inched into the Top 100. As the guys admit, there was no masterplan behind their career; they just tried out different things to see if they worked. Martin-Smith was not a long-serving music business professional (like, say, Pete Waterman, whose influence was at its peak in the late 1980s and

Chapter 3

Take That's Svengali – Nigel Martin-Smith

EVERY POP SENSATION HAS TO have a Svengali behind them. It's part of the unwritten lore. Think of Elvis Presley and Colonel Tom Parker, remember the Beatles and Brian Epstein. For a brief period Andrew Loog Oldham inspired the early Rolling Stones, while Tam Paton controversially did the same for the Bay City Rollers. More recently, there have been Simon Napier-Bell and the Spice Girls matched by Louis Walsh and Boyzone. Nigel Martin-Smith was the Svengali behind Take That.

Born in 1958, Nigel began his career in the early 1980s as a casting agent for theatre, film, television and commercials, based in Manchester's Royal Exchange. He came to believe strongly that the showbiz industry was too focused upon London and that the North West could more than punch its weight in the entertainment field. He was determined to prove his point.

In 1989, he branched out into pop music management, signing up Damian and releasing a version of "The Time Warp" from *The Rocky Horror Picture Show*. Damian had had two earlier stabs at the charts in 1987 and 1988 with "The Time Warp 2", grazing the lower reaches each time. Now, with a remixed take, the song went to Number 7 and stayed in the hit parade for 13 weeks. Nigel is quite proud of the fact that the song still gets played today…although Damian only scored one further Top 50 success with an update of "Wig-Wam Bam", the 1972 smash for glam rockers, the Sweet.

Toe dipped in the water, Nigel now took the chance to prove that Manchester could offer the world a genuine pop boy band and worked hard to put Gary, Mark, Howard, Jason and Robbie together. He then drove them around the UK to gigs, jammed into his Ford Escort. With hindsight, the black leather and studs approach might have been a little rough for a teenage audience, but he learned fast. He didn't really have the in-depth music business experience to handle Take That's career faultlessly, but he did possess a great deal of savvy and enthusiasm, which more than made up for it once their bandwagon had taken off. The results that he achieved as their manager speak for themselves.

It's fair to say that his methods and personality have always sharply divided opinion. At one time, during Take That's glory years in the first half of the 1990s, he was lauded as the most influential gay person in the music industry. Robbie Williams was rather less charitable in his assessment, and others undoubtedly found him a controlling

FAR RIGHT Nigel
Martin-Smith, 2005

figure. But it is undeniable that his vision and effort were instrumental in putting the group together.

When Take That split up, he secured a consultancy deal with Virgin Records and managed the relaunch of Lulu's career, having already given her substantial support when she was invited to sing with the band on their exciting Number 1, "Relight My Fire" (incidentally, despite winning the Eurovision Song Contest with "Boom Bang-A-Bang", and covering David Bowie's "The Man Who Sold The World", her first and only chart-topper).

He also managed the pop music career of Kavana, the stage name of the actor Anthony Kavanagh, who left the TV series, *Coronation Street* in order to release two albums, "Kavana" (1997) and "Instinct" (1999), as well as several singles, notably "Crazy Chance" (written by Howard Donald), a Number 16 hit in 1997, and "MFEO" and "I Can Make You Feel Good", which both went to Number 8 the same year.

Similarly, he managed the transition of former child model and actor Adam Rickitt from *Coronation Street* to pop stardom. Adam's first single, "I Breathe Again" went to Number 5 in the charts, but follow-up singles, "Everything My Heart Desires" and "Best Thing" were less successful, as was the album "Good Times".

In 2005, he was invited to contribute to the TV documentary *Take That – For The Record* as co-producer, and stayed to manage the relaunch of the band's career via the repackaging of their "Ultimate Collection" album and the subsequent sell-out national tour. On the eve of the tour, it was announced the band had once more parted company with their former Svengali, amid frenzied media speculation that such a parting of the ways was opening the door for Robbie Williams to be welcomed back into the fold. This has so far proved a chimera, since Robbie remains resolutely aloof.

Nevertheless, Nigel is generous in his praise of his one-time charges. "I can't believe what a success the comeback has been. I thought they would do the tour and that would be it. But now they could tour every year and pack stadiums."

These days, Nigel divides his time between his many business interests, under the umbrella of NMSM. The company has offices in Nemesis House, Bishopsgate, Manchester from where the Nigel Martin-Smith Management Company continues to seek out new pop music talents. There were recently rumours of a collaboration with Simon Cowell, probably the number one Svengali of today.

There are five other companies run by NMSM. Lime Actors perhaps represents the closest to Nigel's roots in the business, being a management company for professionally trained actors. By contrast, Urban Talent is an agency that looks to discover real people who might turn out to have a natural talent for television.

Smiths Models is a high-fashion model agency that specialises in work at the glamorous end of the spectrum. Nemesis is a model agency which deals with commercial and photographic models at the less rarefied end of the market. Finally, Nemesis Casting is also a close link to his introduction to the showbiz world, dealing in casting for all types, particularly Northern-based extras and walk-ons.

Furthermore, he is the owner of three successful bars on Canal Street, the epicentre of Manchester's gay nightlife. Essential, Queer and Falcon all attract different crowds, the last-named and most recent having a strict men only

policy. In this way, he manages to keep his finger on the pulse of a core interest group.

Chapter 4

The Years of Success 1992 – 1996

FAR RIGHT A visit to New York for the band, who sadly never conquered America

BY THE END OF THE SUMMER OF 1992, the Take That bandwagon was really starting to roll. In August, the album "Take That And Party" was released and peaked at Number 2 in the charts. As well as the singles that had helped to build the group's reputation ("Do What You Like", "Promises", "Once You've Tasted Love" and "It Only Takes A Minute"), three further tracks went on to enjoy success in the hit parade. "I Found Heaven" was released to coincide with the launch of the album and reached a respectable if slightly disappointing Number 15 slot. It was the next three singles that confirmed Take That were here to stay. First, "A Million Love Songs" came out in October and rose to

Number 7, equalling their breakthrough success with "It Only Takes A Minute". Then, crucially, "Could It Be Magic" was released just before Christmas and became the band's first Top 5 success, peaking at Number 3 and remaining in the charts for 12 weeks.

"Could It Be Magic" continued the group's tradition of highly energised cover versions. Written by Barry Manilow, it had been a Top 30 success for him in the UK, 14 years earlier, and, two years before that, a Top 40 success for the female whirlwind, Donna Summer. When "Why Can't I Wake Up With You" was released in February 1993, it reached agonisingly close to the top spot, resting at Number 2. In addi-

RIGHT Another
'Nineties' awards
dinner

tion, the album also contained the title track, "Satisfied", "I Can Make It", "Never Want To Let You Go" and "Give Good Feeling". The nation was partying.

The first major tour to promote this album cemented the group's reputation. On 12 successive days in November 2002, Take That played Newcastle, Bradford, Cambridge, London, Bristol, Portsmouth, Wolverhampton, Manchester, Derby, Scarborough, back to Manchester and York. The concerts were a triumph. Only one thing was missing.

But the first coveted Number 1 hit record was only a whisper away. When "Pray" came out in July, it raced to the top, and was followed there with dizzying speed by "Relight My Fire" (featuring Lulu) in October, "Babe" as the Christmas single and "Everything Changes" in April 1994. Not since the days of the Beatles had a band released four consecutive chart-toppers. Now Take That definitively ruled the singles market, although the spell was fractionally broken when "Love Ain't Here Anymore" only reached Number 3 in July.

Meanwhile the group played nine rapturously received summer concerts at Manchester, Glasgow, Manchester

(again), Birmingham, four nights at Wembley (including an Extravaganza) and the Chelmsford Spectacular.

There could be no gainsaying the group's overall staggering success. The album, "Everything Changes" had raced to Number 1 when it was released in October 1993. Bolstering the six mighty singles ("Why Can't I Wake Up With You" was given another airing), were "Wasting My Time", "If This Is Love", "Whatever You Do To Me", "Meaning Of Love", "You Are The One", "Another Crack In My Heart" and "Broken Your Heart".

The "Everything Changes" tour was their biggest yet. Before Christmas 1993, the group took in three nights at Bournemouth, Cardiff, three at Birmingham, Belfast, Dublin, Brighton, three at Wembley and Manchester, Sheffield, two at Glasgow, Aberdeen and Whitley Bay, provoking widespread pandemonium.

Afterwards, they swept through Europe with two nights in Rotterdam and Brussels, three in Berlin, Kiel, two in Munich, Zurich, two in Dortmund and Frankfurt, Helsinki, Stuttgart, Vienna, two in Milan, Bologna and ending with two in Rome.

Before summer 1994 was over, the group had blitzed the British Isles again. They played four gigs in Glasgow, three in Manchester, two in Dublin, five in Sheffield, two in Cardiff, nine at Wembley and in Birmingham, concluding a punishing tour with two in Belfast.

The rushing vortex of tour, album, tour, album raced on. "Sure" was released as a single in October 1994 and confidently took the Number 1 position. There was a slight gap before "Back For Good", (a song with erroneous intimations of longevity if Take That fans were reading the runes), followed it there in April 1995. Finally "Never Forget" came out in August, by which time the band had been reduced to a foursome.

It was exhausting and it couldn't last. Tempers started to fray within the band,

FAR LEFT The band toured enormously, including Japan

LEFT The group met Princess Diana at the 'Concert of Hope' AIDS benefit in 1994

THE YEARS OF SUCCESS 1992 – 1996

and there were many arguments between band members and the manager. In particular, Robbie Williams and Nigel Martin-Smith were constantly at loggerheads, with Williams chafing at what he considered to be the excessive control placed on the musicians. He flirted very publicly with the Gallagher Brothers, Noel and Liam, the founders of Manchester's other band, Oasis, making it very clear he preferred the indie rock'n'roll lifestyle. He left.

Meanwhile, the third album, "Nobody Else" had also powered to the top of the charts. As well as the three singles and the title track, listings included, "Every Guy", "Sunday To Saturday", "Hanging On To Your Love", "Holding Back The Tears", "Hate It", "Lady Tonight" and "The Day After Tomorrow". The "Nobody Else" tour consisted of ten concerts each in Manchester and at Earl's Court, before the group headed for Adelaide, Melbourne, Sydney, Brisbane and Perth, two nights in Bangkok and Singapore, two in Tokyo and wrapping up in Djakarta.

Rumours were circulating that the remaining members of the band had had enough of life in the goldfish bowl. Fans couldn't believe it, and were temporarily relieved when a press conference was called on 13 February 1996. Surely these stories would now be quashed? But the rumours were true and the break-up was announced with immediate effect.

"We're all a bit nervous," explained Gary, "so if we don't have the answers to your questions we do apologise. Can we just say thanks for everyone's support over the last five years. You've been absolutely fantastic – but unfortunately, the rumours are true… As from today, there's no more. Thank you."

There was only time for a final single, the affecting old Bee Gees song, a Top 3 hit from 1977, "How Deep Is Your Love", released the following month, and a chapter-ending "Greatest Hits" collection which came out in May. Both single and album naturally hurtled to Number 1. Take That were sticking to the great showbiz adage – "always leave the crowd wanting more". But it did seem that it was the end of a fantastic journey.

LEFT Gary Barlow and Howard Donald briefly re-unite, at the 'Party in the Park', 1998

Chapter 5

Robbie Williams

SINCE HE LEFT TAKE THAT IN 1995, Robbie Williams has sold more albums in the UK than any other British solo artist in history – with sales over 53 million worldwide. With his singles being estimated to have sold around 15 million around the world his total sales to date are an estimated 70 million. This is an incredible achievement for the boy from Stoke-on-Trent who began his career with one of the most phenomenal bands of all time.

Born Robert Peter Williams on 13 February 1974, Robbie has simply had one of the most exciting careers of any solo artist in the history of music. His talents don't just include pop – which is where he first found his niche – but comprise a variety of musical styles from adult contemporary to dance, swing, rock and rap. Time and time again, Robbie has proved to those who

doubted that he could make it big time on his own, that he has got what it takes. Continually reinventing himself, Robbie entered the *Guinness Book Of Records* in 2006 when tickets for his world tour went on sale. More than 1.6 million tickets sold in just one day. So what makes this performer such a super star? Well, he's talented, has sex appeal and constantly performs what millions of fans want. He's enthusiastic on stage and interacts with his audience in a way that's personal – he comes across as if he's singing for a whole bunch of mates, rather than a paying crowd.

Between 1998 and 2007 Robbie was the world's best selling male artist with 18 million albums and six million singles sold in the UK alone. The only performer to have more Number 1 albums than Robbie is the legendary "King" of rock'n'roll, Elvis Presley. His status is so

ROBBIE WILLIAMS

high in the UK that he was recently voted into the top five of the Greatest Living Briton Poll. Including his time as a member of Take That, the megastar has sold in excess of 100 million albums, singles and DVDs worldwide since his career began in 1990.

Despite his iconic status, Robbie hasn't always enjoyed the good life. Soon after leaving Take That he battled with drugs and alcohol and was often seen in public looking dirty and dishevelled. He has also had some weight problems which led to Noel Gallagher of Oasis referring to Robbie as: "That fat dancer from Take That" at Glastonbury in 1995. For his part, Robbie had painted a tooth black and dyed his hair peroxide for the event. His reputation in the media wasn't good at the time and many were cynical about his abilities to pursue a solo career. After sorting himself out and a decent shampoo, Robbie was back in 1996 and ready to launch his solo career. His first single was a cover version of the George Michael/Wham! song, "Freedom", which climbed to Number 2, but Robbie needed to clean up his act and went through rehab for drug addiction before releasing a second single.

That turned out to be "Old Before I Die" – a Number 2 in 1997 – taken from his debut album ("Life Thru A Lens") that spawned five singles which would see Robbie heading for the sky. Next followed "Lazy Days" and "South Of The Border" which reached Number 8 and Number 14 respectively, but it was the fourth single harvested from the album that began Robbie-mania.

The emotive "Angels" – voted the best British song of the last 25 years at the 2005 Brit Awards and the one that most people would want played at their funeral – saw the light of day just before Christmas 1997 and peaked at Number 4. It had been claimed that Robbie was sounding too much like an Oasis clone but "Angels" reversed the public's perception of him and began the love affair that continues to this day. The single has since sold more than six million copies worldwide.

Released in March 1998, "Let Me Entertain You" reached Number 3 and Robbie was looking more and more like a success story. But he was finding it hard to break through on the other side of the Atlantic even though in the UK and the rest of Europe he was consistently storming up the charts.

ROBBIE WILLIAMS

RIGHT Robbie has always been a great performer

"I've Been Expecting You" was eagerly awaited and when it was released in 1998 Robbie didn't disappoint as the album merrily sailed to the hot spot in the charts, going on to sell 2.7 million copies in the UK alone. The first single chosen for release was "Millennium" which gave him his first UK chart-topper as a solo artist. It was followed by two Number 4 hits in "No Regrets" and "Strong" before the double A-side of "She's The One"/"It's Only Us" returned him to the top of the charts. (His first two albums were combined and released in the States as "The Ego Has Landed").

"Rock DJ" from the third album, "Sing When You're Winning", had moderate success in the US but the controversial song took Robbie all the way to Number 1 in the UK in 2000. The song itself wasn't the controversial bit; that came with the video in which Robbie strips nude amongst a hoard of female fans. Using CGI technology, the singer is then seen

BELOW Robbie on stage in 2000

ROBBIE WILLIAMS

"stripping" off his skin, muscle tissue and organs which he feeds to the ravenous fans. The skeleton of Robbie dances to the music until the end of the track. It was nominated for an MTV Video Music Award, but the nudity and violence led to a negative public reaction.

He returned to Number 1 in the UK with "Eternity"/"The Road To Mandalay" in 2001, the same year "Swing When You're Winning" – an album of cover versions of songs from the 1950s and 1960s – was released. It is an exciting album that shows off the true extent of the talents of Robbie's voice. Sounding exactly like a crooner from the age of swing, he manages to portray jazz, blues and pop styles of the time. The duet "Something Stupid" (a cover of Frank Sinatra and Nancy Sinatra's original) with Nicole Kidman became a Number 1 Christmas hit in the UK. The follow up album was "Escapology" in 2002 that received mixed reviews. Although the album took Robbie back to a pop-based style he was still struggling to make a breakthrough in the US. The music video did nothing to enhance Robbie's reputation which depicted the singer having three-way sex with two women (although he remained fully clothed). The result was to see his long-term partnership with writing partner, Guy Chambers, come to an end.

The following year saw Robbie playing three consecutive nights at Knebworth in front of a total of 375,000 fans. These events confirmed his status as the most popular solo artist in the country and the album "Live At Knebworth" was released in October and has since gone on to sell around four million copies worldwide.

A "Greatest Hits" compilation was released in 2004 and debuted at Number 1 with more than 320,000 copies flying over the counter in the first week alone. It included two new songs, "Radio" and "Misunderstood", the former giving him his sixth UK chart-topper.

"Intensive Care" came next, three years after its studio predecessor, in a highly-publicised worldwide launch in October 2005. Having partially given up on the US, Robbie announced that the album would not be launched in North America. He changed his mind when demand was such for his latest music and it was released on iTunes on both sides of the Atlantic. It went to Number 1 in the UK and sold an amazing 373,000 copies in its first week, and with

worldwide sales reaching the six million mark it is the singer's fastest selling album. "Sin Sin Sin" was the fourth single released from the album and gave Williams his first taste of life outside the Top 20 when it charted at Number 22. He next released "Rudebox" to mixed reviews in 2006. With collaborations with Joey Negro, The Pet Shop Boys,

LEFT The Live 8 concert in 2005. Robbie performed amongst a host of stars

BELOW Robbie on stage, 2006

RIGHT Robbie in his element, as he performs to a capacity crowd

and William Orbit, amongst others, the album's title track received a damning review from *The Sun* which named it: "The worst song ever" but it did give him his highest US hit to date at Number 19. Gary Barlow – his former bandmate – also felt it wasn't Robbie at his best. He stated that he liked: "Classic Robbie Williams…and this isn't classic…". To date, "Rudebox" is his lowest selling album.

The *Close Encounters World Tour* kicked off in South Africa in April 2006. By the time he had gigged in Europe, Latin America and Australia as well, more than three million fans had been to see him. With rumours that he and Guy Chambers will reunite, Robbie stated that he would release two new studio albums in 2007. Despite his enormous success – or perhaps because of it – Robbie still finds life difficult at times. Between February and March 2007 he entered rehab in Arizona for addiction to the anti-depressant Seroxat. Known to suffer from depression, insecurity and self-loathing, Robbie is loved and adored by literally millions of fans worldwide. It is a shame that this exceptional performer is still unable to love himself.

Chapter 6

Gary Barlow

WITH A CURRICULUM VITAE THAT includes 16 self-penned hit singles during the 1990s, Gary Barlow was surely one of the most talented songwriters of the decade. Born on 20 January 1971 in Frodsham, Cheshire, the exceptionally talented songwriter, singer, pianist and producer entered the BBC's *Pebble Mill At One* "A Song For Christmas" competition with "Let's Pray For Christmas". As a result of making it to the semi-finals, Barlow was invited to record his song in London aged just 15. Inspired and enthusiastic, the young singer decided to try his luck on the northern club circuit with a mix of his own material and cover versions. In 1990 he took on Barry Woolley as his manager but soon came to the attention of Nigel Martin-Smith and became the lead singer of Take That. He was forced to settle out of court with Woolley when his former manager threatened to sue him.

Gary was the first of the previous band members to launch a solo career. His first release "Forever Love" stormed up the charts and gave the singer his first Number 1 single. The album "Open Road" also made it to the top spot and he claimed his second Number 1 single with "Love Won't Wait". Unlike former bandmate Robbie Williams, Gary made it to the charts in the US with "So Help Me Girl" and was followed by a second album "Twelve Months, Eleven Days". Party In The Park, hosted by London's Capital Radio in Hyde Park, featured Gary in both 1998 and 1999. He had been dubbed the greatest songwriter of the 1990s, but the media were ruthless and turned their backs on him at the end of the decade when Robbie began to excel in his own solo career.

LEFT Gary at the 1992
Smash Hits Awards,
where the group won
seven categories

GARY BARLOW

Robbie's "Angels" was the song that would turn the critics against Gary and he found himself with little support from either the media or radio stations. It was a harsh blow for the talented songwriter who had been providing the nation and the world at large with his moving and exciting music.

Maybe cruelly, Robbie made fun of Gary by including the lyrics "Where has Gary Barlow gone?" in a track at the end of his album "Escapology". It was too much for the vulnerable Gary who consigned himself to the recording studio as a writer and producer. He established himself as the President of True North Country Music where to date he has worked with Elton John, Delta Goodrem, Donny Osmond and Christina Aguilera, to name but a few.

However, he wasn't going to hide away forever and when the successful television documentary about Take That was shown to a mass audience it led to the revival of the band. The group re-formed, without Robbie, in 2006 and Gary was back where he belonged – leading the phenomenal band on the road to fame and stardom.

Take That didn't just provide Barlow with a successful five-year career com-

bined with fame and fortune. He also met his wife Dawn Andrews through the band. She was a dancer for Take That and the couple were married in 1999. They have two children: Daniel (born 2000) and Emily (born 2002). His domestic happiness would make Robbie retract his previous taunting of his former friend stating that he would swap his fame and success for Gary's family life. *My Take*, Barlow's autobiography was published by Bloomsbury and first issued in hardback. The paperback which followed included an additional chapter which took the reader up to the present day with his comeback with the band and the up and coming tour planned for late in 2007. Until his autobiography, Gary remained staunchly quiet about himself, despite the huge amounts of media interest and articles that were written about him. In the book, Gary describes the incredible and highs and lows he experienced when Take That split in 1996. He had enjoyed a promising start to his solo career, but then had a crisis of confidence. His once adoring fans had found other singers to fawn over and the hero-worship that had once followed him everywhere was all but gone.

GARY BARLOW

The book also reveals how Gary found life on the road with Take That and his truth about the rumours of the infamous feuds that went on. He starts with his early life, growing up in Cheshire and how his life on the club circuit changed forever when he met Martin-Smith. The singer also tells of the situation when he and Robbie went through a very public falling-out. What does come across from the book is Gary's ever present determination and positive attitude. This spirit has enabled him to make a graceful and timely comeback. Meanwhile, despite his own performing career suddenly taking off again, he has been a successful songwriter for other great artists such as Charlotte Church, Atomic Kitten, Delta Goodrem, H & Claire, Will Young, Amy Studt, Graham Gouldman and Blue.

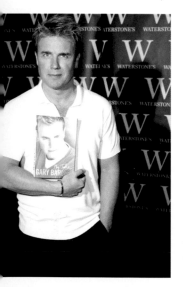

It must have been an amazing feeling for Gary when "Forever Love" made the Number 1 hot spot in the UK charts. It was his

very first solo single. "So Help Me Girl" made the Number 11 slot while "Open Road" the title track from the album made it to the Top 10, peaking at Number 7. "Are You Ready Now" also hit the Top 10 at Number 8 and "Hang On In There Baby" – which was the sixth and final single released from the album – climbed to Number 12. "Stronger" made it to Number 16 in the UK charts while "For All That You Want" peaked just outside the Top 20 at Number 24. Of the 12 titles included on his first solo album, "Open Road", half of them were self-penned numbers. Two others, "My Commitment" and "Lay Down For Love", were collaborations with other songwriters and only four songs were written by others, including Madonna. Released in 1997 it was followed two years later by a second album, "Twelve Months, Eleven Days", which peaked at Number 35 in the UK charts. Even though Gary all but lost his fans when Robbie made it as songwriter and performer nearly 10 years ago, he is back, strong, ready and with his legendary spirit set to continue his huge contribution to the British music scene with the comeback of Take That and their long-awaited tour.

Chapter 7

Mark Owen

BORN IN LANCASHIRE MARK Anthony Patrick Owen was educated in Oldham. He worked in retail and a high street bank before he found his true destiny with Take That in 1990. The road to music couldn't have been further from his dreams of becoming a professional football player. Mark, born on 27 January 1972 had trials for Manchester United, Huddersfield Town and Rochdale but suffered a serious injury that put paid to his first-choice career.

He was the third member of Take That to start a solo career, after Gary and Robbie, and his first solo record, "Child", reached Number 3 in the UK charts. It was followed by a second single, "Clementine", which also peaked at Number 3. His debut album, "Green Man" in 1997, left the singer and songwriter disappointed when it only climbed to Number 33 in the UK album charts. He was dropped by record label BMG Records later the same year when his third single "I Am What I Am" only just made it into the Top 30 at Number 29.

For six years, Mark's life turned in a different direction, but he made a personal comeback on Channel Four's *Celebrity Big Brother* in 2002. He won the second series of the reality show which well and truly returned him to the spotlight. A deal with Island/Universal Records saw him make it back into the charts in August 2003 with "Four Minute Warning", his first single in a number of years which peaked at Number 5. The single stayed in the UK charts in the Top 40 for eight weeks and he followed it up with a second album "In Your Own Time". Released in November 2003, the album reached Number 39 in the charts while

MARK OWEN

the single "Alone Without You" managed the Top 30 where it charted at Number 26. Again, he was dropped by his record label and fed up with being overlooked he created Sedna Records in April 2004. As well as setting up his own company, Mark was also busy writing his own material for his next album. "How The Mighty Fall" was recorded in the States later that year and released in the UK in 2005. The single from the album, "Hail Mary", was eventually released in February 2006. Like Gary, Jason and Howard, Mark was brought back to public attention by the hugely successful television documentary about Take That in 2006. The band's singles "Patience" (released in 2006) and "Shine" (2007) both made it to Number 1 in the UK charts. It was the relaunch that Mark needed and Take That's single "I'd Wait For Life" was released in June 2007 prior to the group's huge tour planned for the end of the same year. In the spring of 2007 there were widespread rumours that Mark would be working on his fourth solo album in the summer of 2007.

In his personal life, Owen dated art student Joanna Kelly after leaving Take That and then lived in the Lake District

with actress Chloe Bailey. Mark and his former girlfriend, actress Emma Ferguson, had a son, Elwood Jack who was born in August 2006. Despite the birth of their son, the couple decided to cancel their marriage plans the same year. But, in December 2006, the couple announced their plans to marry. Just prior to this, Mark had completed a hugely successful tour of the UK at the end of 2003.

Produced by Tony Hoffer, "How The Mighty Fall" was Owen's first album released under his own company, Sedna Records. The album was launched on 18 April 2005 and included the singles; "They Do", "Sorry Lately", "Waiting For the Girl"; "3:15", "Wasting Away", "Stand" and Come On". The other two singles that he released from the album – besides "Hail Mary", included "Makin' Out" which reached Number 30 in the UK charts and "Believe In The Boogie" which didn't fare well when it reached Number 57. Before his collaboration with Hoffer (renowned for his work with Supergrass, the Thrills and Turin Brakes to name but a few), Mark worked with the legendary John Leckie. The producer was responsible for Mark's first album, "Green Man". As one

MARK OWEN

RIGHT Back on stage
in 2006 as a member of
Take That

BELOW Football has
always been a passion
for Mark

of the UK's most prolific and acclaimed producers, Leckie began his career as a tape operator and engineer at Abbey Road Studios.

He worked with George Harrison on "All Things Must Pass" and John Lennon's "Plastic Ono Band" as well as Pink Floyd's "Dark Side Of The Moon". He began in production in the mid-1970s but left Abbey Road to become a freelance producer two years later in 1978. He became renowned for his work with various bands and solo artists and was frequently involved with the likes of Bill Nelson and Simple Minds. He is probably best known for his work with Stone Roses in 1989. As well as working with Owen, Leckie was an instrumental part of the team with the Verve on the album "A Storm In Heaven" and Radiohead's "The Bends".

Mark had approached Leckie about his album because he wanted to portray a closer image to indie Brit-pop than Take That had been known for. Fans and critics alike are waiting to see what the rumoured fourth album will bring. However, the most exciting news is his continued commitment to Take That and the future that the most phenomenal band in music history have to offer.

Chapter 8

Howard Donald

HOWARD DONALD WAS BORN ON 28 April 1968 at home in Droylsden, Manchester to Kathleen and Keith. As time passed, he found himself right in the middle of a fairly large family, with two older brothers, Michael and Colin, a younger brother, Glenn, and a younger sister, Samantha. Perhaps it was this position that lay at the roots of him wanting to be a performer, or perhaps it was the fact that his mother was a singer and his father was a Latin American dance teacher, so it was in his blood anyway.

After attending primary school at Moreside Junior High School in Jorsdan, Manchester, he moved on to Little Moss High School for Boys. Although he passed exams in English, Geography and Mathematics, Howard was by no means a model pupil, preferring to spend his time breakdancing and riding his BMX bike.

His early ambition was to be a pilot but by the time he had left school, he had modified his plans and soon took an apprenticeship with specialist car spraying concern Knibbs in Manchester. He completed his apprenticeship, and got his first full-time job working as a spray painter for Wimpole Garages. Meanwhile, he was continuing to improve his breakdancing and had joined a crew called the RDS Royal.

The RDS Royal used to go to the Manchester Apollo, where the crews tended to congregate. One night, Howard was very impressed with the dancing of a member of the rival Street Machine crew. It was Jason Orange. They later got talking, discovered they felt the same way about a lot of things and had had many similar experiences so they decided to leave their crews, pool their resources and form Streetbeat.

LEFT Howard on stage in 1998

Shortly afterwards, they approached Nigel Martin-Smith to see if he would be interested in being their manager. He was impressed but realised that dancing needed to be allied to singing and song-writing to form the perfect pop package. It just so happened that he had a project forming in the back of his mind. He introduced Howard and Jason to Gary and Mark, who were also on his books. Once Robbie had joined to form the quintet, Take That were up and running.

Although he, Jason and Mark were inevitably confined mostly to backing vocals, chosen for their excellent movement and well-chiselled looks, it was the chemistry of the group that was so crucial. Besides that, he did have occasional moments at the centre of the stage, which proved he could more than carry a tune. In fact, Howard took lead vocals on "If This Is Love", the live version of "Why Can't I Wake Up With You" and, most affectingly, the anthem "Never Forget" that was to prove such a pertinent swansong for the band in its original formation.

After Take That finally split in 1996, Howard was probably the most devastated of all. It didn't help that gremlins

jumped all over his plans when he decided to go solo. He recorded a single, "Speak Without Words", and even got as far as filming a video for it in Cuba before things went wrong at the record company and they decided not to release it. The same neglect was unfortunately foisted upon the album he recorded, about which he reminisces fondly. As a songwriter, he donated the song "Crazy Chance" to Kavana, another of Martin-Smith's solo acts – it made Number 35 in the charts in May 1996 and, re-released in September 1997, rose to Number 16.

He then tried his hand at being a DJ, going out under the name of DJ HD and releasing a single, "Take Control". He rapidly established an appreciative audience in clubs and student unions, particularly in the North West, playing a mixture of "uplifting, chunky house and soulful grooves". His fame then spread to Ibiza, and to the dance floors of Austria, Germany and Switzerland, and on around the world. In fact, he enjoys this type of performing so much and has been so successful at it that he still continues doing it today.

Apart from guesting with Gary at a Prince's Trust concert, he hadn't per-

HOWARD DONALD

formed live on stage for 10 years. Still, he was interested to answer the call for a reunion, however temporary he thought it might be, although he confesses that he has been staggered by the depth of feeling in the response.

"I thought most people had moved on with their lives. I knew there was some interest because we had finished on top, and you still heard the records on the radio, and people sometimes went on about what a good group we were and what a great live act. But I didn't think people would be interested in rushing

out and buying these tickets for a live show. We didn't have that confidence to say let's stick in all these 20 dates at once. We just released a few dates to start with but they sold like hot cakes and we had to release the others straightaway. We were overwhelmed by it all."

By general consent, Howard's interviews in the TV documentary *Take That – For The Record* which inspired the band to re-form were perhaps the wittiest and most trenchant. From comments about the band's notorious first video shoot ("I was cleaning jelly out of my a******* for the next two years") to his self-laceration when he wanted to throw himself in the Thames after the band split ("I wanted to kill myself but I'm just too much of a s******* to do it"), he rivalled the loquacious Robbie for quotability – no mean feat.

As is the way of things, the revived interest in Take That has stimulated even greater interest in his work as a DJ, so he is now probably busier than ever. His solution to marrying his twin careers is to arrange that he performs as a DJ around dates wherever the group plays. He parties on.

Howard is the father of two young daughters, Grace and Lola.

Chapter 9

Jason Orange

JASON WAS BORN IN MANCHESTER on 10 July 1970, along with his twin brother, Justin, to Jenny and Tony. He was one of a large family. As well as his other brothers Simon, Dominic, Samuel and Oliver, he also has two half-sisters, Emma and Amy, a stepbrother, also called Simon, and a stepsister, Sarah.

By his own admission, Jason's schooldays were not exactly overflowing with achievement. He attended primary school at Haveley Hey in Wythenshawe, Manchester, before going on to South Manchester High School. The main things he enjoyed were all non-academic; he liked sports such as football, swimming and athletics. So he left school at the age of 16 with few qualifications and even fewer regrets.

At first, he and Justin joined a local Youth Training Scheme, and he ended up employed as a painter and decorator for an organisation called Direct Works. Jason found this an acceptable way to earn a crust, but he soon decided he didn't want to do it for the rest of his life.

He was really into breakdancing and joined a crew called Street Machine where he soon demonstrated his talents. As a result, he got noticed, and it was not long before he was invited to appear on a TV programme with Pete Waterman and Michaela Strachan, called *The Hit Man And Her*.

Around this time, he met Howard Donald, who was in a rival breakdancing crew. They got on so well that they decided to quit their respective crews and form a new breakdancing duo, Streetbeat. Soon afterwards, they approached Nigel Martin-Smith to see if he would be interested in being their manager. The rest is history.

JASON ORANGE

Although it seemed that, along with Howard and Mark, he was merely there to provide good-looking back-up to Gary and Robbie, the situation was far more complex than that. As subsequent events showed, the chemistry between the band members was of great importance. However, his singing was often the butt of jokes by Gary who once, in response to a request from Jason to write a song for him, said he already had done – but that it was an instrumental.

Jason was hit quite hard by the break-up of Take That, and his entirely natural response was to take a long holiday from showbusiness. He went backpacking around the world for a year or two, during which he learned to mellow out and live a simple life at hostels. The only exceptions where when he was recognised and was forced to check into five star hotels to escape the unwanted attentions of eager groupies.

During his travels, he particularly enjoyed visiting Thailand, Malaysia and New Zealand, keeping a diary of his thoughts before returning home and moving on to New York to enrol in an acting course. When he returned once more to England, Jason found work in

television, playing the part of Brent Moyer, the insidious drug-dealing DJ in the 1999 production of Lynda La Plante's *Killer Net*. He also featured in two plays, firstly in *Let's All Go To The Fair* at the Royal Court Theatre, London, and, more prominently, as the haranguing street-poet in *Gob* by James Kenworth, directed by James Martin Charlton at the King's Head Theatre, also in London.

By all accounts, he turned in professional performances, but he felt he just wasn't cut out to be an actor. Perceptively, he noticed that he always felt as though he was acting, whereas true actors would be actually living the part. It was a boundary that he was going to find difficult to cross. The transition from performing live in front of 20,000 fans and a handful of theatregoers was also hard. So he drifted away from television and the theatre.

This time, Jason decided to rectify the gaps in his education. He enrolled in a course at South Trafford College studying Psychology and Sociology, two subjects that had increasingly fascinated him during his time in the band and thereafter. Although he had now deliberately slipped out of the public eye, he

JASON ORANGE

FAR RIGHT More at home singing, rather that acting

BELOW Jason in 2001

wasn't completely dormant because he still attended charity gigs and functions.

However, when the call came for the group members to work together on a 10th anniversary TV programme, *Take That – For The Record*, he decided he was ready to return to the fray, however briefly. And when the enthusiastic response to the broadcast and the simultaneously released "The Ultimate Collection – Never Forget" meant that a tour was in the offing, he was ready for that as well. But he was very aware that the group would have to take infi-nite pains if they were going to try to interest the public in an album of fresh songs.

With disarming candour, he points out: "You can sell a tour on nostalgia, and we did. But you can't sell new material based on nostalgia – it's got to be quality."

It was. The album, "Beautiful World", more than lived up to expectations. And Jason even got to sing his first lead vocal on the song "Wooden Boat". Fair enough, since he wrote it.

He has a more thoughtful, considered approach to life and music 10 years on, as can be gauged by his involvement in the songwriting labours. It is far less likely, for instance, that he would be unable to remember whether or not he enjoyed the sexual favours of a certain female star.

On the pressures of diving back into the goldfish bowl of superstardom, Jason is more interested in noting his family's reactions. "One or two of them had reservations but the rest were very keen. The first time around my youngest brother was in school and I didn't consider that at the time. It was a real pain for him to have a famous older brother but he's 26 now and it's cool."

Chapter 10

Robbie's Departure & The Break-up

AS IS QUITE COMMON WITH youngsters who have enjoyed incredible success and earned unbelievable sums of money, it doesn't take much for them to go off the rails and that was what seemed to be happening to Robbie in the final 12 months of his Take That career.

He was struggling to control his drink and drug habits which were becoming an embarrassment to the other members of the group. At the Glastonbury Festival in 1995 he was clearly out of control, falling out of a Rolls Royce clutching bottles of champagne and partying with the bad boy of rock, Oasis' Liam Gallagher. Pictures of him were plastered across the newspapers, as

were quotes he had been dishing out in unofficial interviews but he claims to have no memories of the weekend whatsoever.

Rumours soon began to circulate that Robbie was going to leave the group and these were confirmed on 17 July. The official statement read that Robbie "was no longer able to give Take That the commitment they needed" and refunds were offered to fans who had bought tickets for the forthcoming tour with the intention of seeing him.

"The Glastonbury thing was a problem," Mark later explained. "It wasn't why Rob left the band but it did start the break-up. We'd worked for five years and had looked after what was going on

around us – we built a wall around us for five years. You become protective and if people want to do an interview with you they have to go through the proper channels, so what happened at Glastonbury did p**s us off…"

It emerged that there had been tension building between Robbie and Gary, something those in the know had seen looming on the horizon, as A&R man Nick Raymonde explained: "It was always going to be Gary and Robbie that clashed and you could see that was ultimately going to end in tears."

But it also became apparent that Robbie's partying was not received well by the other members of the group and his four band-mates allegedly cornered him one night in rehearsal and said that they were thinking about doing the next tour as a four-piece and asked him for his opinion. Needless to say, Robbie knew he wasn't wanted and departed though he did later admit that he cried because it was over. But he also explained that he had had enough of people's egos and mind games.

Having already completed the recording of their third album "Nobody Else", they could hardly delete Robbie's contribution and the first single, "Never

ROBBIE'S DEPARTURE & THE BREAK-UP

Forget", was released very soon after the split. It became their seventh Number 1 but there wouldn't have been many punters who would have risked their hard-earned cash with a bet that this would be the last release before their farewell offering seven months later. As 1996 began, the press began printing stories that the remaining four members were not going to continue and this was confirmed on 13 February.

It was announced that their cover of the Bee Gees' "How Deep Is Your Love" would be their last single. It was taken from the forthcoming "Greatest Hits" compilation and such was the depth of feeling felt by their fans across the globe that help-lines were set up to help them deal with their devastation.

It was never publicly acknowledged that the reason for their eventual demise was Robbie's departure but Mark did later admit that it was never the same once they had slimmed down to a foursome. Gary and Mark announced their intention to concentrate on their solo careers and nobody categorically stated that the band would never re-form. They appeared at the Brit Awards and played their supposed final gig on 5 April 1996 in Amsterdam.

While Gary was initially quite philosophical about his former band-mate's potential solo success, a verbal war soon grabbed the public's attention. He had admitted prior to the release of "Forever Love" that "Robbie is 10 times more popular than I am. There is no contest. His record is out three weeks after mine. Well, if I'm Number 1 for three weeks I'll be pleased."

Robbie meanwhile was soon engaging in derogatory comments such as "I hate you, Barlow. Gary's selfish, greedy, arrogant and thick. He's a clueless w*****" but he was not totally putting down the Take That songwriter as he did admit "To be honest I know Gary can do better. I know he's got brilliant songs and I know that his album's title track, 'Open Road', is a fantastic song. It's another 'Back For Good', and that was the best song Take That ever did… Gary should have a brilliant solo career. He's a very good songwriter."

It seemed that it would take time to heal the rift between Robbie and the other four members of Take That but Robbie was noticeably absent when Gary, Mark, Jason and Howard did re-form although they had clearly left the door open for him to join them.

Chapter 11

For The Record:
The TV Documentary

"YOU KNOW, OUR DREAM IS THAT after five or 10 years, we'll come back and do it all over again." When Gary said these words at the press conference in Manchester on February 13 1996 to announce that the band were breaking up, he probably had little idea how prescient his thoughts were.

Okay, so five years passed by without a peep, but he was dead right on the second count. Towards the end of 2004, the possibility of relaunching a greatest hits package was mooted and found favour.

So when the idea was first broached to broadcast a TV documentary to mark the 10th anniversary of the break-up of the band, the members were interested but wary. Would it just be an endless series of boring talking heads saying how they loved the band or, alternatively, couldn't stand them? Or maybe just a mindless collection of vaguely amusing stories strung together about young girls getting overexcited at their concerts? Gary, Howard, Jason and Mark decided it wasn't going to be that way.

On the contrary, they agreed, the programme would feature their own recollections of what happened. And, crucially, Robbie declared himself interested. This guaranteed, if guarantee were needed, that there would be no lack of candour in the making of the programme.

Meanwhile, a repackaged greatest hits collection would be released in the same

week. These simultaneous actions would demonstrate whether Take That were still of any relevance to the outside world. It proved to be a marketing masterstroke.

Seven million people watched the broadcast on 16 November 2005. In these days of fragmented TV audiences, this figure far exceeded expectations for a band that had been out of the public eye for such a long time. The story was the key – it was a gripping one. Threading its way through the personalities and the music, it was a classic showbiz tale of rise and fall.

Basically, the documentary told the story of the band from the very early days trekking around the country in Nigel Martin-Smith's beaten-up car. It covered those first concerts and the early videos, before moving on to take in all the trappings of burgeoning success. The cameras took in the pounding excitement of the arena concerts, the almost maniacal reactions of their fans, the security guards fearful for the group's lives (and their own), illuminated in a few short interviews with some of those fans and guards involved.

Mark remembers what the madness was like at its height: "We were heading

LEFT Back in the limelight, Take That pose for the cameras

towards a hotel in Italy. It was off the beaten track but the road at either side was packed with people all chasing the bus. There was a lot of mayhem going on, people were just running down the streets screaming and shouting as we arrived at this hotel with the police escorts. That, for me, summed up what it was like being in that band, with all the travelling around the world, and all the craziness."

The documentary also took in the inevitable decline. It showed the beginnings of the rebellion against managerial rule, some of the intra-band rivalry, Robbie's drinking and drugs binges, his departure from the band, the tight-lipped conviction that "the show must go on", the final tour, the even more final break-up. There was also footage of four of the band (Robbie didn't make it) meeting up in a hotel to discuss old times, like members of a successful football team or veteran soldiers.

Despite not turning up for the reunion, Robbie was still able to provide good copy. On Nigel Martin-Smith: "He's definitely in the top three most disturbed individuals I've ever worked with. I only ever wanted him to love me. That's the really sad thing. And he never

did." The former Svengali metaphorically shakes his head. On wanting to leave the group, Robbie explains he had

for calling Gary a crap songwriter. At the reunion, the other four mumble about what a hard time he had of it.

What set the programme apart was the excellent backstage footage, where little seemed to have been censored and the banter sizzled to and fro. Take That had dared to offer the audience a full measure of honesty and realism, and they were duly rewarded for taking what is often seen as a sizeable risk.

Not only was it a highly rated critical success, but it also registered very strongly with their fans. It's quite possible that maybe they saw another side to the band, and liked what they saw.

The other side of the marketing equation had proceeded according to plan. "The Ultimate Collection – Never Forget" had been released in the same

BELOW 'The Ultimate Tour' was a sell-out

his head up his own backside at the time. He tells Howard, Jason and Mark what good guys they are. He apologises

week as the TV show. It rapidly rose to Number 2 in the album charts. The band were back in the news.

Nominated for an Award in the Arts and Specials Category of the Rose d'Or (the Golden Rose) held in Lucerne in April 2006, the documentary's life continued. When the DVD was released in the same month with obligatory extra footage, it sold exceptionally well.

Also in that same month, the group began "The Ultimate Tour" (which has happily proved to be a misnomer, since it has not turned out to be their last) – an Arenas and Stadiums Tour of the British Isles, which included six shows at Wembley Arena and at Birmingham NEC, three at Manchester MEN Arena, two each at Dublin's The Point, Glasgow SECC (Armadillo), Newcastle Metro and Sheffield Hallam Arena, and a visit to the Odyssey Arena in Belfast.

The stadium shows comprised two each at the Milton Keynes National Bowl and the City of Manchester Stadium, as well as trips to the Millennium Stadium in Cardiff and the RDS Stadium in Dublin.

The hysteria, albeit a little more controlled this time around, was happening all over again.

LEFT The boys backstage at Wembley Arena, 2006

Greatest Hits

THESE DAYS, IT SEEMS THAT anyone can put together a greatest hits compilation even if they've only released a couple of albums. In the early days of such projects, bands often had to wait nearly 10 years before their record company would consider such a proposal. Indeed, Queen issued eight albums before their first "Greatest Hits" was released in 1981.

Of course, if a band decides to call it a day then their record company will quickly cash in on their popularity before it fades and this was the case with Take That. Not that the group's popularity has faded at all in the intervening years as their re-formation has proved. Just three months after the announcement that shocked their fans, RCA Records released a compilation of Take That's hits that stormed to the top of the UK charts.

"Greatest Hits"
Highest UK chart position: Number 1
Year: 1996
Containing all of their single successes – including the US version of "Love Don't Live Here Anymore" – "Greatest Hits" has sold more than a million copies in the UK alone.

"Never Forget – The Ultimate Collection"
Highest UK chart position: Number 2
Year: 2005
This was basically the same as the previous compilation but also included a live version of "Pray" and a remix of "Relight My Fire". It was also notable for the inclusion of a new track, "Today I've Lost You". This was originally written as the follow-up to "Back For Good" but was never released after the group disbanded. The track was recorded in September 2005 for

LEFT Take That sang many of their Greatest Hits on their 'Ultimate Tour'

this album and was then performed on The Ultimate Tour with Gary's wife, Dawn, dancing on stage. The album – which has also sold more than a million copies in the UK – reached Number 2 in the chart and was accompanied by a DVD featuring videos of the songs.

"The Platinum Collection"
Highest UK chart position: Number 2
Year: 2006

November 2006 saw the re-release of "Take That And Party", "Everything Changes" and "Nobody Else" with bonus tracks to coincide with the group's return. These three albums were also combined in a three-disc box-set, "The Platinum Collection", which offered fans who already owned the CDs the chance to buy something a little bit different. Three tracks were added to their debut offering – "Waiting Around", "How Can It Be" and "Guess Who Tasted Love (Edit)" – while their 1993 release was extended by four tracks ("No, Si Aqui No Hay Amor", "The Party Remix", "All I Want Is You" and "Babe (Return Mix)"). The bonus tracks on the third disc were two remixes of "Sure" and "Back For Good" along with a live version of "Every Guy".

LEFT Take That savouring the thrill of performing 'live' again

Chapter 13

The Autumn Tour 2007

AND SO THE WHEELS OF THE mighty circus began to turn in earnest once more. Towards the end of February 2007, the band announced they would be undertaking a major European and UK tour near the end of the year. They would hone their "Beautiful World" stageshow to perfection on a tour of Australia, Canada and Japan during the summer.

As a taster for the tour, the group appeared at the Concert for Diana on 1 July 2007 at Wembley Stadium to mark 10 years since the Princess of Wales died in a car crash in Paris. The concert was held on what would have been her 46th birthday. Members of the group rescheduled time off to fit in the show, because, according to Mark: "Diana was an inspiration to so many people and we feel privileged to have met her." The group once took tea with her at Kensington Palace, which Mark cites as a highlight of their career. "We decided we wanted to do anything we can to make Diana's concert one of the highlights of the summer."

The group kick off their series of shows on Sunday 14 October and Monday 15 October in the Odyssey Arena, Belfast. A short European tour is scheduled to follow with concerts in Barcelona, Spain on Saturday 20 October, in Milan, Italy on Wednesday 24 October, in Vienna, Austria on Friday 26 October, at the Hallenstadion in Zurich, Switzerland on

LEFT Gary in full flow

Saturday 27 October, in Cologne, Germany on Monday 29 October and in Hamburg, Germany on Wednesday 31 October. They then play at the Ahoy in Rotterdam, Holland on Thursday 1 November, in Stuttgart, Germany on Saturday 3 November, in Berlin, Germany on Sunday 4 November, in Frankfurt, Germany on Tuesday 6 November, in Oberhausen, Germany on Wednesday 7 November, at the Gigantium in Aalborg, Denmark on Friday 9 November and at the Forum in Copenhagen, also in Denmark on Sunday 11 November.

All 22 dates for the following two months' tour in the UK sold out in record time, so the band were rapidly compelled to add six extra dates to their already hectic schedule. They were at the NEC in Birmingham from Thursday 15 November to Tuesday 20 November (no show on the Sunday). Here the five shows sold out completely within an hour. After this, they move up to Scotland to play Glasgow SECC from Thursday 22 November to Saturday 24 November before returning to England to play Newcastle Arena on Monday 26 November and Tuesday 27 November.

LEFT Mark, who will have his own lead singing duties on the forthcoming tour

The whistle-stop tour then turns south to take in the O2 Arena (formerly the Millennium Dome) in London from Thursday 29 November to Tuesday 4 December (again, no show on the Sunday), with extra dates added on Thursday 6 December, Friday 7 December and Saturday 8 December. Finally, the band have set up a triumphant homecoming to Manchester with concerts at the MEN Arena from Monday 10 December to Wednesday December 19 (yet again, no show on the traditional day of rest). New shows have been added to cope with exceptional demand on Friday December 21, Saturday December 22 and Sunday December 23.

What can fans expect from the shows? Obviously this will be their first chance to hear the new songs from "Beautiful World" live, including the hit singles "Patience", "Shine" and "I'd Wait For Life". There will be no shortage of ready takers for the songs. When the album was released, it racked up 1.3 million sales in just five weeks, including 437,000 in the Christmas week alone (the highest in that week for 10 years). In fact, in those five weeks, it became the Number 2 selling album for the whole of 2006.

Apart from that, the mixture will probably be not entirely dissimilar to what has gone before, albeit with various subtle changes. The group has such a fantastic back catalogue that no-one will be disappointed.

Before the shows, the atmosphere will build and build until the tension is

LEFT The O2 Arena – still under construction

sweeping ballads. The audience will be dancing to their hearts' content one minute, and rapt in attention the next. Every song will be memorable in its own way.

Gary may handle the majority of the lead singing duties but Mark will sing lead vocal on "Shine", Jason will take the lead on "Wooden Boat" and Howard will come to the fore for "Never Forget". And maybe that hologram of Robbie will reprise his lead vocal on "Could It Be Magic" – provided the man himself can't be coaxed back to appear in person, of course.

The excitement will be intense from start to finish. The only unsurprising thing will be that there will be surprises. But the core of the show will be the same. Mark recalls looking out from behind the curtain before their first concert in Newcastle last year, seeing all the fans who had arrived hours before the start, banners aloft. "We knew we wanted to give people two hours of enjoyment in which they could just forget about their lives." The ideal recipe for perfect entertainment, in other words.

After all, why mess with a winning formula?

ready to snap. The costumes will be stylish, the stage sets will be dazzling, the pyrotechnics will be state of the art. The stage show will be as dynamic as they come, with a plethora of breathtaking moments and effects. The sound will be superb, with the electrifying uptempo dance numbers balanced by the

Never Forget – The Stage Musical

YOU KNOW WHEN YOU'VE MADE a lasting impression on the world when your songs are turned into a musical. The likes of Queen (*We Will Rock You*), ABBA (*Mamma Mia!*), Rod Stewart (*Tonight's The Night*) and Buddy Holly (*Buddy The Musical*) have been honoured in this fashion and 2007 saw Take That join this elite group when *Never Forget – The Take That Musical* received its premier at the Millennium Centre in Cardiff on 20 July.

Although originally the idea of the band's concert choreographer Kim Gavin, Danny Brocklehurst – creator of hit shows such as *Shameless* and *Clocking Off* – was the man responsible for writing the musical which is based around a fictional Take That tribute band. Set in Manchester – where else! – the musical follows hero Ash through highs and lows with his best friends in a feel-good comedy of love, friendship, ambition and betrayal. It was never intended to be a biographical story but it is packed full of hits including "Pray", "Relight My Fire", "Babe", "Back For Good" and, of course, "Never Forget" that were officially licensed by EMI for the show before Take That's 2006 comeback.

It was directed by Ed Curtis (*Conspiracy* and *Marlon Brando's Corset*), choreographed by Karen Bruce (*Footloose* and *Fame*) and co-produced by Tristan Baker, whose credits include

Kiss Me Kate, Little Shop Of Horrors and *Calamity Jane.* After its stint in Cardiff, the musical then visited Glasgow (King's Theatre), Manchester (Opera House), Stoke-on-Trent (Regent Theatre) and Edinburgh (Playhouse) before heading off to London's West End.

"We are creating a spectacle which will appeal to both Take That fans and musical theatregoers alike," explained co-producer Bronia Buchanan. "We hope that the band will be delighted with the production when they see the show themselves."

While the real Take That might well have been impressed with the show if and when they eventually saw it, stories surfaced in April 2007 that legal action was being considered to prevent the musical from going into production. Gary, in particular, was very derogatory about the project claiming "I'm furious and I'll do everything legally possible to stop the show, which has the smell of the end of a pier about it."

"We are the biggest fans of Take That's music," Baker countered, "and we are so excited about the wonderful opportunity to create a new musical based on the fantastic catalogue of their work. We look

forward to creating a legacy with these well-loved songs in the way that shows such as *Mamma Mia!* have done before."

In the end, the band distanced themselves from the production with a state-

ment on their official website that read "There have been reports in the press about a Take That musical. The band would like to state categorically that this production is being undertaken with neither their involvement nor their endorsement. They would wish their fans and the general public to know that this production is absolutely and 100% nothing to do with Take That."

Chapter 15

The Singles

WHEN "EVERYTHING CHANGES" made its UK chart debut at Number 1 in 1994 it gave Take That the distinction of being the first act since the Beatles, almost 30 years earlier, to register four consecutive chart-toppers. By the time their farewell offering – "How Deep Is Your Love" – entered at the top of the chart two years later, they had become the first artists to see their singles hit the peak of the chart in the first week of release.

"Do What You Like"
Highest UK chart position: Number 82
Year: 1991
Co-written by Ray Hedges and Gary Barlow – who also contributed the lead vocals – "Do What You Like" was the group's debut release but it flopped. Nigel Martin-Smith had selected this track from "Take That And Party" but

sales were hindered by a cheesy video which saw half-naked band members rolling around in jelly that has since been voted the second worst video of all time by VH1.

"Promises"
Highest UK chart position: Number 38
Year: 1991
Again written by the Hedges-Barlow partnership, "Promises" proved to be the first Take That single to hit the Top 40. The band members jumped on Robbie's hotel bed so much once they heard the news that it broke.

"Once You've Tasted Love"
Highest UK chart position: Number 47
Year: 1992
Their third offering from their debut album failed to improve on the success

of its predecessor. With Gary on lead vocals and Robbie rapping in an attempted American accent, this proved to be the last single that failed to make the Top 15.

"It Only Takes A Minute"
Highest UK chart position: Number 7
Year: 1992

Despite Gary's reluctance to release a cover, Take That's rendition of Tavares' US Number 1 hit from 1975, the disco beat of "It Only Takes A Minute" – with the video featuring the dancing skills of Howard and Jason in particular – found a willing audience in 1992 and saw them register their first Top 10 entry.

"I Found Heaven"
Highest UK chart position: Number 15
Year: 1992

The first Take That single on which Robbie got to perform the lead vocals was also the first release not penned by Gary. It was, in fact, written by producers Ian Levine and Billy Griffin, and set the stage for the release of their debut album.

"A Million Love Songs"
Highest UK chart position: Number 7
Year: 1992

Recorded in just one take, "A Million Love Songs" had been written by Gary many years earlier and established his

LEFT Singing all their hits, Take That in 2006

reputation as one of the best songwriters in Britain in the early 1990s.

One of three songs written by Gary at the age of 16, "Why Can't I Wake Up With You" was only kept off the top of

"Could It Be Magic"
Highest UK chart position: Number 3
Year: 1992

Another cover version was the final release from the boys' debut album and this time it was a Barry Manilow classic from 1975. "Could It Be Magic" saw Take That register their highest chart position to date and it won Best British Single at the Brit Awards.

"Why Can't I Wake Up With You"
Highest UK chart position: Number 2
Year: 1993

the chart by 2 Unlimited's dance hit "No Limit".

"Pray"
Highest UK chart position: Number 1
Year: 1993
It was another Barlow composition that gave Take That their first UK chart-topper. "Pray" hit Number 1 in July 1993 and was the first release from their second studio offering "Everything Changes".

"Relight My Fire"
Highest UK chart position: Number 1
Year: 1993
A collaboration with Lulu saw a second consecutive Number 1 single for Take

That and a first for the 1960s songstress. The original plan had been for Robbie to partner Lulu on lead vocals on the Dan Hartman composition, but this was ditched as Gary's voice combined perfectly with the Scot.

"Babe"
Highest UK chart position: Number 1
Year: 1993
With lead vocals from Mark, "Babe" was the answer to everyone's prayers when it knocked Mr Blobby off the top of the chart. Unfortunately for everyone over the age of six, Noel Edmunds' annoying pink creation exacted revenge and claimed the Christmas Number 1 the following week.

THE SINGLES

RIGHT Take That, backstage at the Royal Variety Performance in 2006

for two weeks. Take That were by now the biggest act in the UK.

"Love Ain't Here Anymore"
Highest UK chart position: Number 3
Year: 1994

This was Take That's only single in a three-year period (1993-96) that failed to hit Number 1. Not surprisingly, really, when you consider that Wet Wet Wet's "Love Is All Around" – the theme from the hit movie *Four Weddings And A Funeral* – was enjoying a four-month stay at the top of the charts!

"Sure"
Highest UK chart position: Number 1
Year: 1994

With lead vocals from Gary, Robbie and Mark, "Sure" was the first offering from Take That's third studio album "Nobody Else". It also returned the boys to the top of the chart after the hiccup of "Love Ain't Here Anymore".

"Everything Changes"
Highest UK chart position: Number 1
Year: 1994

The fifth single from the album of the same name again saw the group at the summit of the charts where it remained

"Back For Good"
Highest UK chart position: Number 1
Year: 1995

Such was the demand for this single, that its release date was advanced by six weeks. Written in just 15 minutes by

Gary, it sold 300,000 copies in the first week of sales and became the band's first US Top 10 hit.

"Never Forget"
Highest UK chart position: Number 1
Year: 1995
This was the final Take That single to feature the vocal talents of Robbie, who had left the band just a couple of weeks before its release. It featured home videos of the band members as children and was produced by the legendary Jim Steinman.

"How Deep Is Your Love"
Highest UK chart position: Number 1
Year: 1996

The quartet's farewell single was a cover of the Bee Gees' 1977 Number 3 hit "How Deep Is Your Love". It performed better than the original, however, giving

THE SINGLES

Take That their eighth UK chart-topper and went on to sell more than 500,000 copies.

"Patience"
Highest UK chart position: Number 1
Year: 2006
A return to form after a 10-year hiatus, "Patience" is credited to all four band members plus producer John Shanks. It went on to become the eighth best-seller of the year and won the boys another Brit Award for Best British Single.

"Shine"
Highest UK chart position: Number 1
Year: 2007

The second single to be released from their comeback album "Beautiful World", "Shine" – featuring Mark on lead vocals – matched the chart success of its predecessor to become Take That's 10th Number 1 hit.

"I'd Wait For Life"
Highest UK chart position:
(released 18 June)
Year: 2007
With Gary returning to the lead vocal role, the video for "I'd Wait For Life" was a far cry from their light-hearted beginnings. Premiered on Channel 4 a month before the single's release, it showed the foursome having flashbacks following an accident.

Chapter 16

The Albums

DESPITE THE FACT THAT TAKE That only released three albums between their arrival on the scene in 1991 and their split five years later, their sales figures stand at an incredible nine million copies worldwide. When their comeback offering "Beautiful World" was released in 2006 to rave reviews and huge success, it merely confirmed what their fans have always recognised. Take That are quite simply one of the biggest acts that the UK has produced in the last 20 years.

"Take That And Party"
Highest UK chart position: Number 2
Year: 1992
Released in September 1992, "Take That And Party" debuted in the UK charts at Number 5 before peaking at Number 2 despite competition from Mike Oldfield's "Tubular Bells II", and great-

est hits compilations from Kylie Minogue and ABBA. The album spent a staggering 73 weeks in the charts and went on to sell more than 750,000 in the first 12 months. It succeeded all expectations as Nigel Martin-Smith had claimed that to achieve a gold disc for 100,000 copies sold would be a fantastic result, but the mixture of ballads and dance tunes proved to be a perfect recipe for success.

"Everything Changes"
Highest UK chart position: Number 1
Year: 1993
The band's second studio album picked up where its predecessor had left off,

dethroning Meat Loaf's "Bat Out Of Hell II – Back Into Hell" from the top of the charts on 23 October 1993. Sadly, Take That's stay in the peak position only lasted seven days as the American gained his revenge the following week. With the album containing four Number 1 hits, it's no wonder that more than 300,000 copies flew off the shelves in the first week of release. A more mature mix of songs, it was also notable for "If This Is Love" which was Howard's first published foray into songwriting.

"Nobody Else"
Highest UK chart position: Number 1
Year: 1995

Released in May 1995 – just a month after the departure of Robbie Williams – "Nobody Else" spent two weeks at Number 1 and put fans' fears to rest that Take That had nothing left to offer. The artwork and the majority of the recording had already been completed before the group slimmed down to a foursome so it was decided to issue it with Robbie's contributions in place. Despite containing the Number 1 hits "Sure", "Back For Good" and "Never Forget", the album's sales fell short of "Everything Changes" but it did give the band their first US chart entry…albeit at a lowly Number 69.

LEFT Take That at the
2006 Q Awards

THE ALBUMS

RIGHT The band launching 'Beautiful World' in 2006

"Beautiful World"
Highest UK chart position: Number 1
Year: 2006

The first new Take That album in a decade was eagerly anticipated and when it was released in November 2006 it didn't disappoint. "Beautiful World" was a departure from their previous offerings in that each of the four members sang lead vocals on at least one track, although Gary still claimed the lion's share of this task with six of the 12 songs. The album was extremely well received by critics and fans alike and has since sold more than two million copies worldwide.

RIGHT Take That performing 'Shine', with Gary at the piano

Also available:

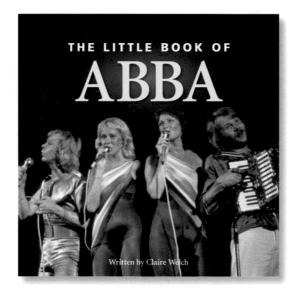

Available from all major stockists or online at:
www.greenumbrellashop.co.uk

The pictures in this book were provided courtesy of the following:

GETTY IMAGES
101 Bayham Street, London NW1 0AG

PA PHOTOS
www.paphotos.com

Creative Director, Design and Artwork: Kevin Gardner

Published by Green Umbrella Publishing

Publishers Jules Gammond and Vanessa Gardner

Written by Ian Welch, Claire Welch and Mike Hobbs